easy sous vide

4 simple steps to delicious meals

edited by Mary Dan Eades

photography by Mehosh Dziadzio

Paradox Press

contents

22
beef

34
pork

introduction

Chefs have embraced the sous vide cooking technique for decades, but for most home cooks, it's completely new. Novelty aside, however, the very reasons that it has become the go-to method for chefs are exactly what make it perfect for the average cook at home. It's foolproof. It's simple. It's almost entirely hands-off. And it produces results that cannot be achieved by any other cooking method: food of incomparable taste and texture, cooked to perfection, without shrinkage or loss of nutrients.

Cooking the sous vide way requires no skill—the machine does the work perfectly—and only a few simple steps that even a beginning cook can master immediately and do in minutes. As with any new way of cooking, there are some differences and a few rules you'll want to learn, and we'll cover those momentarily, but first let's look at how easy and foolproof it is to cook this way. Here is all you have to do:

1 : Season
Season the food lightly with salt, pepper, and herbs or spices, if desired.

2 : Seal
Vacuum seal the food in a food-grade cooking pouch.

3 : Simmer
Drop the sealed pouch into a preheated water bath, at the temperature specified in the recipe, for the required amount of time. The food cannot overcook even if you forget about it. You simply cannot ruin a meal.

4 : Serve
Many foods can be plated directly from the pouch. If a golden brown, crisp exterior is preferred—for roasts, poultry, steaks, and chops—give the food a brief finishing sear (on the grill, under the broiler, in a hot skillet, or using a kitchen torch) before serving.

The beauty of sous vide cooking is that it allows you to adjust your cooking to your schedule instead of your schedule to your cooking, and this book will show you how to do just that. Each section begins with an easy sous vide recipe, followed by recipes for simple serving variations. From one sous vide poultry recipe, for example, you can cook an easy family meal and have additional portions ready to make future quick and delicious recipes. Here's how it works.

Cook multiple meals at the same time

You can cook many portions of a given food simultaneously in a water oven, and since it takes no longer to cook one serving than many, you can easily cook enough for a week or more of meals at once, then refrigerate or freeze them for use later. The vacuum-sealed pouch will keep the food fresh for days in the refrigerator and protected from freezer burn until you are ready to use it weeks—or even months—later. (See pages 59 and 60 for tips on quick chilling and vacuum sealing liquid or liquid rich foods.)

By cooking multiple portions of staple foods, such as meat, poultry, fish, seafood, fruits, and vegetables in advance, you can mix-and-match later to quickly turn them into a wide variety of delicious meals in less hands-on time than you'd spend driving through the fast food lane or dining out.

Here's how easy it is:

Cook: Cook multiple portions of staple foods—chicken breasts, for instance—at one time. The prep will take you only a few minutes and the cooking itself is completely hands-off. You don't even have to be there.

Serve or Save: When cooked, sear some of the chicken to serve with vegetables and a salad one night, and refrigerate or freeze the rest.

Make Meals in Minutes: Those saved staples will be ready and waiting to be turned—with just a few minutes of hands-on time—into many different and delicious meals. In our example, the cooked chicken breasts quickly become Chicken Teriyaki with Bok Choy and Mushrooms (page 20), Chicken Marinara with Penne Pasta (page 21), or Chicken with Artichoke Hearts, Sun-dried Tomatoes, and Spinach (page 19). Likewise, you can turn cooked flank steak into Steak Fajitas (page 28), Beef and Noodle Salad (page 27), or Vegetable Beef Soup (page 29). The possibilities are limitless.

Set the temperature and let the water oven do the rest

In traditional cooking, perfect results depend on perfect timing and skill to know exactly when to remove the food from the heat. A moment's distraction can ruin a steak or burn the vegetables. In sous vide cooking, on the other hand, timing isn't critical, because perfect results depend not on time but on precise temperature control, which requires no skill on the part of the cook. With just the push of a button anyone can set the temperature control of the water oven precisely. Foods can be cooked at their perfect serving temperature and held for extended periods of time without loss of flavor or appeal.

The amount of time the food must cook before it can be served depends on the thickness and tenderness of the food in the pouch. The minimum amount of time needed to bring a given food to its target temperature throughout depends on its thickness, regardless of the type of food. For example, a 1-inch (2.54 cm) steak or chicken breast will be heated through to its target temperature in about 1 hour. Once a food has been brought to its target temperature throughout, it's cooked. The reason some recipes call for longer sous vide cooking times (flank steak or tri-tip, for example) is because extended time tenderizes the food.

The magic of sous vide is that food can never overcook, no matter how long you leave it in the water bath at its target temperature. Once heated through, if it's an already tender food—fish, beef and pork tenderloin, lamb chops, fruits, or vegetables—it's ready to eat. Extending the cooking time from that point on will only tenderize the food. Tougher foods—roasts, ribs, game, grass-fed meats, and inexpensive cuts of meat—benefit from that added time to become fork tender. Long, slow cooking can turn the most pedestrian cut of meat into something sublime. And remember, the water oven does the work for you. It's completely hands off.

Here's all you'll need to get started:

A sous vide water oven—one of the self-contained SousVide Supreme™ appliances—or an immersion circulator and a water tub, or another reliable system to precisely control the temperature of a water bath.

Food grade plastic pouches, certified by their manufacturer as suitable for cooking, and a means to vacuum seal the pouches: a suction vacuum sealer, chamber vacuum sealer, or zip-pouch vacuum sealer.

~ Mary Dan Eades, Editor

chicken

chicken leg quarters sous vide

Serves 4
Hands-on time: 10 minutes
Sous vide cooking time: 2 to 4 hours

4 chicken leg quarters
salt and black pepper to taste
high-smoke-point oil (grapeseed, peanut, vegetable, lard)

1

Fill and preheat the water oven to 176°F (80°C).
▶ Rinse the chicken and pat dry.
▶ Season the chicken to taste with salt and pepper.

2

Put the leg quarters into cooking pouches and vacuum seal.
▶ Arrange the pouches in a rack to separate them during cooking.

3

Submerge the pouches in the water bath and let simmer for at least 2 hours and up to 4 hours.
▶ If not using right away, quick chill (page 59).
▶ Remove the leg quarters from the pouches and pat dry. Reserve the liquid stock for another use, if desired.

4

Pour enough oil into a heavy skillet to cover the bottom, and heat on high until it just begins to smoke.
▶ Sear the chicken until it's a light golden brown (about 30 seconds per side).
▶ Serve with your choice of vegetables, starch, or salad.

chicken and wild rice salad

Serves 4
Hands-on time: 10 minutes
Cooking time: 60 minutes

2 Chicken Leg Quarters Sous Vide (page 12), unseared

½ cup (3.25 oz/92 g) long grain rice

½ cup (3.05 oz/86 g) wild rice

3 cups (720 ml) chicken broth

2 ribs celery, trimmed and chopped

4 green onions, trimmed and chopped

1 cup (4 oz/110 g) green peas, thawed

½ cup (1.75 oz/50 g) pecan pieces

½ cup (2.6 oz/75 g) dried cherries

salt and pepper to taste

For the dressing:

2 tablespoons (30 ml) white wine vinegar

1 teaspoon (5 ml) sugar (or ½ packet artificial sweetener)

salt and pepper to taste

3 tablespoons (45 ml) olive oil

1 tablespoon (15 ml) dark sesame oil

Pull the meat from the leg quarters, dice it, and discard the bones. Set aside.

Put the rice and chicken broth into a saucepan and bring to a boil. ▶ Reduce the heat to low, cover, and cook for 40 minutes. ▶ Remove from heat, drain, and cool completely.

Make the dressing: in a bowl, whisk together the vinegar, sugar, salt and pepper. ▶ Let sit for a few minutes, then whisk in the olive and sesame oils.

In a large bowl gently mix together the chicken, cooled cooked rice, chopped celery, green onions, peas, dried cherries, pecans, and dressing. ▶ Adjust seasonings with salt and pepper to taste. ▶ Serve.

chicken bow tie pasta with tarragon-mustard cream sauce

Serves 4
Hands-on time: 10 minutes
Cooking time: 30 minutes

2 Chicken Leg Quarters Sous Vide (page 12), unseared

1 pound (16 oz/454 g) bow tie pasta (farfalle)

1 teaspoon (5 ml) salt for pasta water

1 tablespoon (15 ml) extra-virgin olive oil

½ pound (8 oz/227 g) white mushrooms, thinly sliced

1 large shallot, peeled and minced

¾ cup (6 fl oz/180 ml) dry white wine

1¼ cups (10 fl oz/300 ml) chicken stock

½ cup (4 fl oz/120 ml) heavy cream

2 tablespoons (30 ml) coarse-grained mustard

salt and pepper to taste

2 tablespoons (30 ml) chopped tarragon

Bring a large pot of water to a boil on the stove. ▶ Add 1 teaspoon salt and pour in the bow tie pasta. ▶ Cook for 8 to 10 minutes.

Meanwhile, remove the skin from the leg quarters, pull the meat from the bones and slice; discard bones and skin.

Warm the olive oil in a skillet over medium high heat. ▶ Add the mushrooms and cook over high heat, stirring occasionally, until browned, 4 to 5 minutes. ▶ Add the shallot and cook, stirring, for 2 minutes. ▶ Add the wine and cook until reduced to 2 tablespoons (30 ml), about 4 minutes. ▶ Add the stock, cream and mustard and bring to a boil. Reduce heat to simmer and cook until the sauce has reduced by half, about 6 minutes, stirring occasionally.

Add the chicken to the skillet and warm through, if needed; season with salt and pepper. ▶ Stir in the tarragon.

Drain the bow tie pasta well. ▶ Add to the skillet, tossing to combine and coat with the sauce. ▶ Serve with a green salad and crusty bread.

chicken breasts sous vide

Serves 4
Hands-on time: 15 minutes
Sous vide cooking time: 2 to 4 hours

4 chicken breast halves, boneless and skinless
salt and black pepper to taste
high-smoke-point oil (grapeseed, peanut, vegetable, lard)

1

Fill and preheat the water oven to 146°F (63°C).
▶ Rinse the chicken breasts and pat dry.
▶ Season to taste with salt and pepper.

2

Rolling the ends under to make the breasts an even thickness, put them into a cooking pouch and vacuum seal. (Or vacuum seal the breasts in smaller portions and arrange the pouches in a rack to separate them during cooking.)

3

Submerge the pouch in the water bath and let simmer for at least 2 hours and up to 4 hours.
▶ If not using right away, quick chill (page 59).
▶ Remove the chicken from the pouches, and pat dry. Reserve the liquid stock for another use, if desired.

4

Pour enough oil into a heavy skillet to cover the bottom, and heat on high until it just begins to smoke.
▶ Sear the chicken until it's a light golden brown (about 30 seconds per side).
▶ Serve with your choice of vegetables, starch, or salad.

chicken with artichoke hearts, sun-dried tomatoes and spinach

Serves 4
Hands-on time: 5 to 10 minutes
Cooking time: 30 to 35 minutes

4 Chicken Breasts (halves) Sous Vide (page 16), sliced
1 to 2 tablespoons (15 to 30 ml) olive oil
1 jar (8.5 oz/241 g) sun-dried tomatoes, in oil, minced
1 clove garlic, peeled and minced
1 can (14 oz/400 g) artichoke hearts, quartered
1 package (7 oz/198 g) baby spinach

In a skillet, add the olive oil and heat to medium. ▶ Sauté the garlic in the oil until it's fragrant. ▶ Add the sun-dried tomatoes, including their oil, and simmer for about 15 minutes. ▶ Add the artichokes and simmer for another 10 minutes.

Just before serving, add the baby spinach to the pan and toss until it's slightly wilted.

Put a portion of the mixture onto each plate, along with the sliced chicken breasts.

chicken teriyaki with bok choy and mushrooms

Serves 4
Hands-on time: 5 to 10 minutes
Cooking time: 10 to 15 minutes

4 Chicken Breasts (halves) Sous Vide (page 16), sliced

2 tablespoons peanut oil or other high-smoke-point oil

2 cloves garlic, peeled and minced

4 heads baby bok choy, washed and leaves separated

8 ounces (227 g) trumpet mushrooms, or sliced crimini mushrooms

salt and pepper to taste

1 tablespoon (15 ml) sake (Japanese rice wine)

2 tablespoons (30 ml) mirin (sweet rice wine)

3 tablespoons (45 ml) soy sauce

1 teaspoon (5 ml) brown sugar

2 cups cooked rice for serving

In a wok or skillet heat the oil and sauté the garlic until fragrant. ▶ Add the mushrooms and bok choy and stir-fry until tender. ▶ Season with salt and pepper to taste. ▶ Remove with a slotted spoon to a serving bowl and cover to keep warm.

To make the teriyaki sauce, pour the rice wine, mirin and soy sauce into the skillet and bring to a simmer over medium heat, stirring occasionally. ▶ Add the brown sugar and continue to cook until the sauce has slightly thickened.

Add the sliced chicken to the pan and coat with the teriyaki glaze. ▶ Serve with the bok choy and mushrooms, and cooked rice.

chicken marinara with penne pasta

Serves 4
Hands-on time: 5 to 10 minutes
Cooking time: 20 to 25 minutes

2 Chicken Breasts (halves) Sous Vide (page 16), sliced

1 pound (16 oz/454 g) penne pasta

2 teaspoons (10 ml) coarse salt

2 tablespoons (30 ml) olive oil

½ small onion, peeled and minced

1 clove garlic, peeled and minced

1 tablespoon (15 ml) fresh flat leaf parsley leaves, coarsely chopped

4 or 5 large fresh basil leaves chopped, or 1 teaspoon (5 ml) dried basil

1 can (15 oz/425 g) tomato sauce

½ cup (4 fl oz/114 ml) red wine

freshly ground pepper to taste

freshly grated Romano cheese, for serving

Bring a large pot of water to a boil and add 1 teaspoon (5 ml) salt. ▶ Drop the penne into the water and cook for 7 to 10 minutes until al dente.

Meanwhile, in a large skillet, warm the olive oil over medium heat and saute the onion until soft, about 5 minutes. ▶ Add the garlic and parsley and cook a few minutes more. Stir in the basil and 1 teaspoon (5 ml) salt. ▶ Add the tomato sauce and red wine, stirring to combine.

Raise the heat to high and bring the mixture to a boil. ▶ Reduce the heat to low, cover, and simmer for 15 minutes. ▶ Add black pepper and adjust salt to taste.

Add the sliced chicken to the sauce and warm it through, if needed.

Drain the pasta well, add it to the skillet, and toss to coat with the sauce. ▶ Top with freshly grated Romano cheese, and serve with crusty bread and a salad.

beef

24
easy cooking instructions for
flank steak sous vide

flank steak sous vide is used in:

27
beef and noodle salad

28
steak fajitas

29
vegetable beef soup

30
easy cooking instructions for
tri-tip roast sous vide

tri-tip roast sous vide is used in:

32
firehouse chili

33
philly cheese steak sandwiches

flank steak sous vide

Serves 4
Hands-on time: 15 minutes
Sous vide cooking time: 8 to 24 hours

1½ to 2 pounds (24 to 32 oz/700 to 907 g) flank steak
salt and pepper to taste
1 tablespoon butter, lard, or rendered bacon fat (optional)
high-smoke-point oil (grapeseed, peanut, vegetable, lard)

1

Fill and preheat the water oven to your preferred degree of doneness for steak: 120°F (49°C) for rare; 134°F (56.5°C) for medium-rare; 140°F (60°C) for medium; 150°F (65.5°C) for medium-well.
▶ Rinse the meat and pat dry.
▶ Season to taste with salt and pepper.

2

Put the steak (and fat, if using) into a cooking pouch and vacuum seal. (Or cut the steak into smaller serving sizes, vacuum seal in separate pouches, and arrange the pouches in a rack to separate them in the water bath.)

3

Submerge the pouch in the water bath and let simmer for at least 8 hours and up to 24 hours.
▶ If not using right away, quick chill (page 59).
▶ Remove the steak from the pouch and pat dry. Reserve the liquid stock for another use, if desired.

4

Pour enough oil into a heavy skillet to cover the bottom, and heat on high until it just begins to smoke.
▶ Sear the steak until it's nicely browned (about 30 to 40 seconds per side).
▶ Serve with your choice of vegetables, starch, or salad.

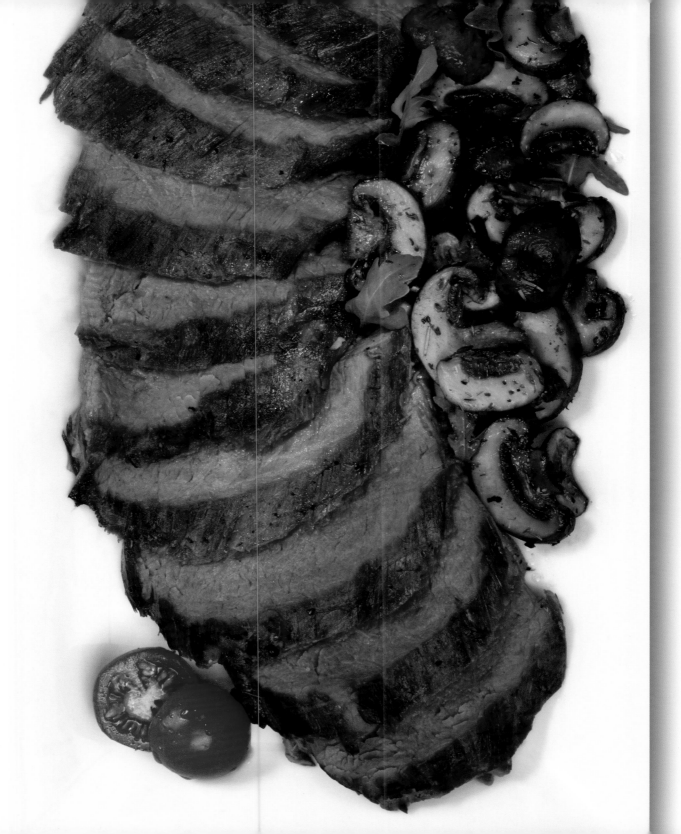

beef and noodle salad

Serves 4
Hands-on time: 10 minutes
Cooking time: 15 minutes

1 pound (16 oz/457 g) Flank Steak Sous Vide (page 24), thinly sliced

1 pound (16 oz/454 g) dried rice noodles

1 tablespoon (15 ml) peanut oil

½ cup (1 oz/25 g) carrots, peeled and cut into matchstick pieces

2 cloves garlic, peeled and finely chopped

1 teaspoon (5 ml) freshly grated ginger root

3 scallions, trimmed and sliced into matchstick pieces

1½ cups (3.5 oz/100 g) bok choy, coarsely chopped

3 tablespoons (45 ml) soy sauce

1 bunch fresh cilantro

Soak the noodles in a large bowl of just-off-boiling water until soft. ▶ Drain the noodles and cool to room temperature.

In a large skillet or wok, heat the oil and stir fry the carrots. ▶ Add the garlic, ginger and scallions and continue to cook for 30 seconds. ▶ Add the bok choy and cook until wilted, about 2 minutes. ▶ Stir in the soy sauce, and remove from the heat.

Add the noodles and sliced beef to the skillet and toss with the stir-fry mixture. ▶ Transfer to a serving dish and garnish with fresh cilantro leaves. Serve chilled or at room temperature.

steak fajitas

Serves 4
Hands-on time: 10 to 15 minutes
Cooking time: 10 to 15 minutes

1 pound (16 oz/457 g) Flank Steak Sous Vide (page 24), sliced in 2-inch (5-cm) pieces
3 tablespoons (45 ml) fajita seasoning*
¼ teaspoon cayenne pepper (optional) to taste
olive oil, as needed
1 red bell pepper, stemmed, cored, and sliced
1 green bell pepper (or poblano chile) stemmed, cored, and sliced
1 small red onion, peeled and sliced
8 to 12 flour tortillas, warmed
4 tablespoons (60 ml) sour cream
fresh cilantro for garnish

Combine the dry seasonings and spices in a large bowl, add 3 tablespoons olive oil, and stir. ▶ Add the flank steak pieces and toss to coat with the seasoned oil.

Put 2 tablespoons of olive oil into a large skillet over medium heat and sauté the peppers and onions until tender, about 8 to 10 minutes. ▶ Remove the vegetables to a bowl and keep warm. ▶ Raise the heat and add the seasoned steak to the skillet to sear and warm through, a minute or two, if needed.

Serve the steak and vegetables with warm tortillas, sour cream, and cilantro.

*Buy ready-made fajita seasoning or make your own with 1 tablespoon (15 ml) chili powder, 2 teaspoons (10 ml) paprika, 1 teaspoon (5 ml) salt, 1 teaspoon (5 ml) sugar, ½ teaspoon (2.5 ml) cumin, ½ teaspoon (2.5 ml) onion powder, ¼ teaspoon (1.25 ml) garlic powder.

vegetable beef soup

Serves 4
Hands-on time: 10 to 15 minutes
Cooking time: 20 to 25 minutes

1 pound (16 oz/457 g) Flank Steak Sous Vide (page 24), cut into pieces

2 tablespoons (30 ml) olive oil

2 cloves garlic, peeled and minced

1 small sweet onion, peeled and diced

1 carrot, peeled and diced

1 zucchini squash, trimmed and diced

1 yellow Italian squash, trimmed and diced

½ teaspoon (2.5 ml) sea salt, or to taste

½ teaspoon (2.5 ml) onion powder

½ teaspoon (2.5 ml) Herbes de Provence

¼ teaspoon (2.5 ml) black pepper

¼ teaspoon (1.25 ml) cayenne pepper to taste (optional)

1 can (14.5 oz/411 g) diced tomatoes

1 quart (32 fl oz/0.9 liters) beef stock

1 handful fresh flat leaf parsley, chopped

In a soup pot, warm the olive oil over medium heat and sauté the garlic, onion, and carrot until soft. ▶ Raise the heat to medium-high, add the squashes, and brown slightly, stirring often. ▶ Add all remaining ingredients, except parsley, and bring just to a boil.

Reduce the heat and simmer the soup for 10 to 15 minutes.

Ladle into bowls, top with some fresh parsley, and serve with warm rolls and butter.

tri-tip roast sous vide

Serves 6 or more
Hands-on time: 5 to 7 minutes
Sous vide cooking time: 8 to 24 hours

2 pounds (32 oz/907 g) tri tip roast
salt and pepper to taste
½ teaspoon garlic powder, optional
high-smoke-point oil (grapeseed, peanut, vegetable, lard)

1
Fill and preheat the water oven to your preferred degree of doneness for beef: 120°F (49°C) for rare; 134°F (56.5°C) for medium-rare; 140°F (60°C) for medium; 150°F (65.5°C) for medium-well.
▶ Rinse the meat and pat dry.
▶ Lightly season with salt, pepper, and garlic powder, if using.

2
Put the roast into a cooking pouch and vacuum seal.

3
Submerge the pouch in the water bath and let simmer for at least 8 hours and up to 24 hours.
▶ If not using right away, quick chill (page 59).
▶ Remove the roast from the pouch and pat dry. Reserve the liquid stock for another use, if desired.

4
Pour enough oil into a heavy skillet to cover the bottom, and heat on high until it just begins to smoke.
▶ Sear the roast on all sides until it's nicely browned (about 1 minute per side).
▶ Serve with your favorite vegetables, starch, or salad.

firehouse chili

Serves 8
Hands-on time: 10 to 15 minutes
Cooking time: 20 to 30 minutes

1 pound (16 oz/457 g) Tri-tip Roast Sous Vide (page 30), diced into ½-inch (1.25-cm) pieces

3 tablespoons (45 ml) rendered bacon fat or oil

1 medium onion, peeled and diced

2 cloves garlic, peeled and minced

2 tablespoons (30 ml) chili powder

1 tablespoon (15 ml) smoked paprika

1 tablespoon (15 ml) ground cumin

1 teaspoon (5 ml) garlic powder

1 teaspoon (5 ml) onion powder

1 can (4 oz/113 g) mushroom stems and pieces, drained

1 can (14 oz/397 g) dark red kidney beans, drained

1 can (4 oz/113 g) fire-roasted, diced green chiles, mild or hot

1 can (28 fl oz/828 ml) tomato sauce

1 quart (32 fl oz/0.9 liters) beef broth

4 dashes Tabasco hot pepper sauce, or to taste

8 tablespoons (2 oz/60 g) grated cheddar cheese

Warm the fat or oil in a soup pot over medium heat. ▶ Saute the onions and garlic until translu-cent. ▶ Add the diced tri-tip and all the dry seasonings and stir to coat the meat.

Add the mushrooms, kidney beans, chiles, tomato sauce, and beef broth. ▶ Raise the heat to medium-high and bring the mixture just to a boil. ▶ Reduce heat and simmer for 10 to 15 min-utes, or until ready to serve.

Taste for heat level and adjust with additional hot pepper sauce, if desired. ▶ Garnish with cheddar cheese, and serve with crackers and butter.

philly cheese steak sandwiches

Serves 4
Hands-on time: 15 minutes
Cooking time: 20 minutes

1 pound (16 oz/457 g) Tri-tip Roast Sous Vide (page 30), sliced very thin or chopped

2 tablespoons (60 ml) olive oil

1 medium onion, peeled and sliced

1 bell pepper, stemmed, cored, and sliced

8 provolone cheese slices

mayonnaise (optional)

4 hoagie buns, split and toasted

In a large skillet or griddle, heat the oil and sauté the onion and pepper slices. ▶ When the veggies are tender, add the sliced beef and warm through. ▶ Top with the cheese, cover and allow the cheese to melt for a minute or two.

Spread some mayonnaise onto each bun, divided the meat mixture evenly, and serve.

pork

36

easy cooking instructions for

pork tenderloin sous vide

pork tenderloin sous vide is used in:

pork tenderloin sous vide

Serves 4
Hands-on time: 6 to 8 minutes
Sous vide cooking time: 1½ to 4 hours

2 pork tenderloins, 1½ to 2 pounds
(24-to 36-oz/684- to 912-g)
salt and pepper to taste
¼ teaspoon (1.25 ml) garlic powder

¼ teaspoon (1.25 ml) onion powder
1 tablespoon (15ml) rendered bacon fat, butter, or lard (optional)
1 stem fresh sage (optional)
high-smoke-point oil (grapeseed, peanut, vegetable, lard)

1

Fill and preheat the water oven to your preferred degree of doneness for pork: 134°F (56.5°C) for medium-rare; 140°F (60°C) for medium; 150°F (65.5°C) for medium-well.
▶ Rinse the meat and pat dry.
▶ Sprinkle all over with salt and pepper, and with the garlic and onion powder, if using.

2

Put the tenderloins and sage and fat, if using, into cooking pouches and vacuum seal.

3

Submerge the pouches in the water bath and cook for 1½ to 2 hours or up to 4 hours.
▶ If not using right away, quick chill (page 59).
▶ Remove the meat from the pouch and pat dry. Reserve the accumulated liquid for another use, if desired.

4

Pour enough oil into a heavy skillet to cover the bottom, and heat on high until it just begins to smoke.
▶ Sear the pork tenderloins on all sides until they are a light golden brown (about 30 seconds per side).
▶ Serve with your favorite vegetables, starch, or salad.

barbecue pork sandwiches with creamy cole slaw

Serves 4
Hands-on time: 5 to10 minutes
Cooking time: 10 minutes

1 pound (16 oz/457 g) Pork Tenderloin Sous Vide (page 36), chopped

1 cup (8 fl oz/236 ml) commercially-prepared barbecue sauce, plus extra for serving

4 large, toasted burger buns

2 cups (24 oz/680 g) cabbage slaw mix (or shredded cabbage)

For the cole slaw dressing:

2 tablespoons (30ml) mayonnaise

1 teaspoon (5 ml) Dijon mustard

2 tablespoons (30 ml) white wine vinegar

1 teaspoon (5 ml) sugar (or ½ packet artificial sweetener)

¼ teaspoon (1.25 ml) celery seeds

In a saucepan, warm the barbecue sauce, add the chopped pork, and heat through for about 5 minutes.

Combine all ingredients for the **cole slaw dressing** in a large bowl. ▶ Add the cabbage slaw mix and toss to coat evenly with the dressing.

Brush some barbecue sauce on the bun bottoms, pile on a scoop of barbecued pork, some slaw, and the top bun. ▶ Serve with baked beans, and chips or fries, if desired.

pork and vegetable stir-fry with hoisin sauce

Serves 4
Hands-on time: 10 to 15 minutes
Cooking time: 15 to 20 minutes

1 pound (16 oz/457 g) Pork Tenderloin Sous Vide (page 36), sliced into strips

2 tablespoons (30 ml) vegetable oil

1 garlic clove, peeled and chopped

2 celery stalks, cut into matchsticks

3 medium carrots, cut into matchsticks

4 scallions, trimmed and cut into matchsticks

2 tablespoons (30 ml) cornstarch, mixed into ¼ cup (2 fl oz/60 ml) water to dissolve

1 bunch fresh cilantro, chopped

cooked rice or noodles, prepared according to package directions, for serving

For the sauce:

2 tablespoons (30 ml) soy sauce

2 tablespoons (30 ml) hoisin sauce

1 tablespoon (15 ml) chili sauce

2 tablespoons (30 ml) dry sherry

Make the sauce: In a small bowl, combine the soy, hoisin, and chili sauces with the sherry, and set aside.

Heat the oil in a wok or skillet until it sizzles. ▶ Add the chopped garlic and stir-fry for 1 minute. ▶ Add the celery and carrots, and stri-fry for 2 minutes. ▶ Add the scallions, and stir-fry for 1 minute more before adding the sauce mixture. ▶ Bring to a boil, reduce the heat to low, cover, and simmer for 2 to 3 minutes, until the vegetables are cooked.

Whisk in the cornstarch mixture, continuing to simmer until the sauce has thickened. ▶ Add the pork tenderloin strips and toss to coat with the sauce.

Serve with rice or noodles, garnished with chopped cilantro.

pork tenderloin with fettuccini and pesto cream sauce

Serves 4
Hands-on time: 10 to 15 minutes
Cooking time: 20 minutes

1 pound (16 oz/457 g) Pork Tenderloin Sous Vide (page 36), sliced

1 pound (16 oz/454 g) fettuccini

1 tablespoon (15 ml) salt

½ cup (4 fl oz/120 ml) heavy cream

2 tablespoons (30 ml) butter

¼ cup (0.9 oz/25 g) grated Parmesan cheese

For the pesto:

1 cup (2.67 oz/75 g) fresh basil leaves

¾ cup (2.67 oz/75 g) grated Parmesan cheese

4 tablespoons (60 ml) pine nuts

3 cloves garlic, peeled

salt and pepper, to taste

3 fluid ounces (90 ml) extra virgin olive oil

Bring a large pot of water to boil. ▶ Add the salt and drop in the fettuccini. ▶ Cook for 8 to 10 minutes, until al dente.

Meanwhile, make the pesto: Put all ingredients for the pesto, except the olive oil, into the food processor and pulse to chop. ▶ With the motor running, stream in the olive oil. ▶ Set aside.

Warm the cream in a large saucepan. ▶ Add the butter and let it melt. ▶ Add the pesto and stir to combine. ▶ Stir in the grated parmesan cheese. ▶ Add the sliced pork, coat with the sauce, and let it warm through, if needed.

Drain the pasta well, add it to the pan with the pork and pesto cream sauce, and toss to coat. ▶ Serve with salad and garlic bread sticks.

salmon

44
easy cooking instructions for
salmon fillets sous vide

salmon fillets sous vide are used in:

salmon fillets sous vide

Serves 4
Hands-on time: 15 minutes
Sous vide cooking time: 20 to 30 minutes

4 salmon fillets (4 oz/113 g each), pin bones and skin removed
salt and pepper to taste
1 lemon, sliced thinly
4 sprigs fresh dill (optional)

1

Fill and preheat the water oven to your preferred degree of doneness for fish: 116°F (47°C) for rare; 126°F (52°C) for medium-rare; 140°F (60°C) for medium.
▶ Rinse the fillets and pat dry.
▶ Season with salt and pepper to taste.

2

Put the fillets, in a single layer and presentation side down, into cooking pouches. Lay a couple of lemon slices and a sprig of dill on the bottom of each fillet.
▶ Vacuum seal the pouches.
▶ Arrange the pouches in a rack to seperate them during cooking.

3

Submerge the pouches in the water bath and let simmer for 20 to 30 minutes.
▶ If not using right away, quick chill (page 59).

4

Remove the fillets from the pouches, pat dry, and serve with your choice of vegetables, sauces, starches, or salad.

greek salmon

Serves 4
Hands-on time: 5 minutes
Cooking time: 0 minutes

4 Salmon Fillets Sous Vide (page 44)
1 pint (300 g) cherry or grape tomatoes, halved
1 cucumber, diced
2 ounces (60 g) pitted Kalamata olives
12 to 15 fresh mint leaves
2 tablespoons (30 ml) olive oil
1 lemon, for juice
coarse salt and ground pepper
mixed greens for serving
4 ounces (113 g) feta cheese, coarsely crumbled

Combine the tomatoes, cucumber, olives, mint, and olive oil in a bowl. ▶ Squeeze the lemon over the top, season with salt and pepper to taste, and toss.

Arrange the mixed greens on a serving plate and top with the salmon. ▶ Spoon the tomato mixture over the fish and sprinkle with the feta.

Serve accompanied by a dry white wine or black tea over ice.

grilled salmon caesar salad

Serves 4
Hands-on time: 5 to 10 minutes
Cooking time: 10 minutes

4 Salmon Fillets Sous Vide (page 44)

high-smoke-point oil (grapeseed, vegetable, or peanut)

balsamic vinegar

1 head romaine lettuce, washed and chopped

1 ounce (30 ml) shaved Parmesan cheese

8 to 10 croutons, crushed (optional)

For the salad dressing:

juice of 1 lemon

1 clove garlic, minced finely or pressed

4 anchovy fillets or 1 to 1½ teaspoons (5 to 7.5 ml) anchovy paste

1 tablespoon (15 ml) mayonnaise

1 tablespoon (15 ml) Dijon-style mustard

1 tablespoon (15 ml) Worcestershire sauce

Make the salad dressing: Put the juice of the lemon into a shallow bowl. ▶ Add the garlic and anchovy fillets and mash with two forks until you've got a smooth paste (or use anchovy paste). ▶ Add the remaining ingredients and mix with a fork to blend thoroughly.

Toss the romaine with the dressing to coat all the lettuce evenly. ▶ Add the Parmesan and croutons and toss again.

Heat an oiled grill pan or skillet to high heat. ▶ Brush the salmon fillets with the oil and vinegar and sear briefly on one side to form a light golden crust, about 2 minutes.

Divide the salad among four serving plates, top with the salmon fillets, and enjoy.

salmon with spinach rice and raisins

Serves 4
Hands-on time: 5 to 10 minutes
Cooking time: 35 minutes

4 Salmon Fillets Sous Vide (page 44)
1 cup (6.5 oz/184 g) long-grain white rice
coarse salt and ground pepper
1 bag (7 oz/198 g) fresh spinach leaves washed well and coarsely chopped
For the sauce:
1 tablespoon (15 ml) olive oil
3 fluid ounces (90 ml) dry white wine
2 ounces (60 g) pitted Kalamata olives, slivered
¼ cup (0.8 oz/25 g) golden raisins

In a medium saucepan, bring 1¾ cups water to a boil. ▶ Add the rice, season with salt, and return to a boil. ▶ Reduce to a simmer, cover, and cook just until tender, about 20 minutes.

Remove the pan from the heat; add the spinach, cover, and let stand, without stirring, for 5 minutes. ▶ Using a fork, fluff the rice and mix in the spinach.

While the rice is cooking, **make the sauce:** Heat the oil in a large skillet over medium heat. ▶ Add the olives and raisins and sauté for 1 to 2 minutes. ▶ Add the wine, and cook over medium-high heat until almost evaporated, 1 to 2 minutes.

Serve the salmon over spinach rice, and top with sauce.

vegetables

52

easy cooking instructions for

vegetables sous vide

vegetables sous vide are used in:

vegetables sous vide

Serves 4
Hands-on time: 5 to 10 minutes
Sous vide cooking time: 30 to 90 minutes

1 pound (16 oz/454 g) vegetables, washed and peeled, if necessary
salt and pepper to taste
1 to 2 tablespoons (15 to 30 ml) butter (optional)
fresh or dried herbs of choice (optional)

1

Fill and preheat the water oven to 183°F (83°C).
▶ Cut large vegetables into 1-inch (2.5-cm) pieces or less for even cooking. Ears of corn can be left whole.
▶ Season lightly with salt and pepper, and the fresh or dried herbs.

2

Put each type of vegetable in a single layer into separate cooking pouches.
▶ Add the butter, if using, and vacuum seal.
▶ If cooking more than one type of vegetable, arrange the pouches in a rack to separate them during cooking.

3

Submerge the pouches in the water bath.
▶ Cook tender vegetables (asparagus, broccoli, cauliflower, eggplant, fresh beans and peas, peppers, summer squash) 30 to 45 minutes.
▶ Cook tougher vegetables (beets, carrots, corn, potatoes, turnips, winter squash) 60 to 90 minutes.
▶ If not using right away, quick chill (page 59).

4

Open the pouch and serve, or use in other recipes.

vegetable risotto

Serves 4
Hands-on time: 5 minutes
Sous vide cooking time: 45 minutes

1 pound (16 oz/454 g) Vegetables Sous Vide (page 50) cut into bite-size pieces

For the risotto:

1 cup (3 oz/90 g) Arborio rice

½ teaspoon (2.5 ml) butter

½ cup 92 oz/59 g) diced pancetta (optional)

3 cups (24 fl oz/720 ml) vegetable, mushroom, or chicken broth

2 cans (4 ounces/113 g each) mushroom stems and pieces, chopped

1 sprig fresh rosemary leaves, minced

salt and pepper to taste

freshly grated Parmesan cheese, for serving

Put all the **risotto ingredients** except cheese into a zip-closure cooking pouch. ▶ Follow the instructions on page 60 for sealing the pouch.

Submerge the pouch in the water bath and cook for 45 minutes. (The risotto can be cooked during the last 45 minutes of the vegetables' cooking time.)

Open the risotto pouch, and fluff the rice with a fork. ▶ Divide the vegetables among 4 bowls. Top with the risotto, and sprinkle with Parmesan cheese.

Variation: Combine 1 cup of Basmati rice and 2 cups of liquid (water or broth) in a zip-closure cooking pouch, and follow the instructions on page 60 for sealing the pouch. Submerge the pouch in the water bath and cook for the last 40 minutes of the vegetables' cooking time. Serve with the vegetables, topped with a sprinkle of sesame seeds and soy sauce.

vegetable curry

Serves 4
Hands-on time: 5 minutes
Cooking time: 10 minutes

1 pound (16 oz/454 g) Vegetables Sous Vide (page 50) and cut into bite-size pieces

3 tablespoons (45 ml) vegetable oil

1 medium onion, peeled and finely chopped

4 hot chili peppers, stemmed, seeded, and finely chopped

2 cloves garlic, peeled and finely chopped

1 teaspoon (5 ml) ground coriander seed

2 teaspoons (10 ml) ground cumin

½ teaspoon (2.5 ml) ginger powder

1 teaspoon (5 ml) turmeric

4 teaspoons (20 ml) tomato paste

1 teaspoon (5 ml) garam masala

½ cup (4 fl oz/114 ml) heavy cream

1 can (15 oz/425 g) chickpeas (garbanzo beans)

salt and pepper to taste

fresh chopped cilantro for serving

Heat the oil over medium heat, add the onions, and stir-fry until tender. ▶ Add the chili peppers and stir-fry for a few more minutes. ▶ Reduce the heat to low, add the garlic and cook for another minute. ▶ Stir in the coriander, cumin, ginger and turmeric until the mixture is thoroughly blended.

Add the tomato paste and garam masala and mix well. ▶ Add the cream a little at a time, stirring constantly until the sauce is an even consistency and heated through.

At the end of the cooking time, add the vegetables and chickpeas to the curry. ▶ Season with salt and pepper to taste and garnish with chopped cilantro. ▶ Serve accompanied by a green salad and naan (Indian flatbread).

pasta primavera

Serves 4
Hands-on time: 5 minutes
Cooking time: 15 minutes

1 pound (16 oz/454 g) Vegetables Sous Vide (page 50) and cut into strips
(carrots, asparagus, bell peppers, zucchini, and summer squash work well in this dish)
1 pound (16 oz/454 g) spaghetti or fettuccini
salt and pepper to taste
freshly greated Parmesan cheese for serving
For the sauce:
1 large tomato, diced, with its juice
1 large bunch of basil leaves, cut into ribbons
½ cup (4 fl oz/114 ml) olive oil

Combine all sauce ingredients in a small bowl. ▶ Set aside to marinate at room temperature for at least 15 minutes.

Bring a large pot of water to a boil. ▶ Add a little salt and the pasta, and cook until it can be cut cleanly with a fork, about 10 minutes.

Drain the pasta well and transfer to a serving bowl. ▶ Add the vegetables and toss with the sauce. ▶ Top with the Parmesan cheese and serve.

Variation: To make an antipasto, dice the vegetables, combine with the sauce and serve cold or at room temperture with crusty Italian bread.

sous vide basics

Cooking *sous vide* (a French term meaning *under vacuum*) involves vacuum-sealing a given food—meat, fish, poultry, vegetables, fruit—in a food-grade pouch and submerging it in a temperature-controlled water bath for as long as it takes to bring the food to the desired temperature throughout. Food cooks gently and precisely and cannot overcook, since it can only reach the temperature of the water in the bath. Flavor and moisture that would normally escape into the air or drip into the pan stay locked in the food pouch, which produces the most flavorful, tender, and juicy food possible.

Chef George Pralus developed the technique in France about 40 years ago as a method for perfectly cooking and minimizing the costly shrinkage of foie gras. Chef Bruno Goussalt popularized the technique by introducing it in the first-class cabin cuisine on Air France's international flights. Since then, it has become a favored cooking technique of great chefs around the globe and the secret weapon of chefs in competitions.

The introduction in 2009 of the SousVide Supreme, the first water oven designed for kitchen countertops, made the technique practical for everyone, from the rank novice to the accomplished cook.

How does sous vide cooking work?

Unlike traditional cooking methods, such as roasting, broiling, grilling, or sautéing that use aggressively high temperatures to heat the air around the food, the sous vide technique relies on the superior ability of water to transfer heat to the food. Because the transfer of heat through water is many times faster than the transfer of heat through air, removing all, or at least most, of the air from the cooking pouch—creating the vacuum seal— is important, as pockets of air between the pouch and the food can result in uneven cooking.

When cooking sous vide, the water bath temperature is set at precisely the desired target for doneness—for instance, 146°F (63.5°C) for perfectly done chicken breasts. Foods cook gently for (at a minimum) long enough to allow the heat of the water to penetrate to the center of the food. How long that process takes has been carefully worked out mathematically for a wide variety of food types, and depends not as much on the weight of the food being cooked as on its thickness. For example, if it takes 40 minutes to bring a piece of chicken that is one-inch thick to temperature, it might take four hours to bring a two-inch thick piece to that temperature. It is important, for food safety, to carefully adhere to the minimum cooking times and holding instructions.

The simple steps of sous vide cooking

Season your food lightly with salt and pepper, or fresh or dried herbs and spices.

Seal the food in an appropriate sized food-grade cooking pouch. Use the vacuum-seal option for most foods, and the seal-only option for foods containing more than just a tablespoon of liquid. Use zip-closure cooking pouches and Archimedes' Principle (page 60) for foods containing a substantial amount of liquid.

Simmer the food at the desired temperature in the preheated water bath for at least the minimum recommended amount of time to ensure it is heated to the center. In most cases, you can leave the food in the water bath substantially longer without loss of quality.

Sear or sauce your food, if desired. All foods that have been cooked sous vide will be delicious straight from the pouch, but some benefit from a complementary sauce or a quick sear in a hot skillet, on a grill, or with a kitchen torch to impart the expected crisp, golden crust and savory flavor.

Basic rules of easy sous vide cooking

Group foods together according to the temperatures that they cook. Red meats (steaks, burgers, lamb) can all cook at the same temperature to your preferred degree of doneness: rare, medium-rare, medium, medium-well. White meats (chicken or turkey breast and pork chops, ribs, or roasts) can all cook at one temperature. Chicken, turkey or duck thighs and legs cook hotter—176°F (80°C)—and longer, so they're a breeze to do overnight. Fruits and vegetables of every type can cook at the same temperature—in the range of 180°F (82°C) to 185°F (85°C)—simultaneously in about 30 minutes to an hour-and-a-half, depending on their tenderness or toughness.

The length of cooking required depends on two things: thickness of the food in the pouch and its tenderness or toughness. Tender cuts merely need to be brought to the desired temperature—perhaps 45 minutes to an hour for a 1-inch piece of steak or a burger—then given a finishing quick sear. Though they may be heated through in the same hour, long, slow cooking of tougher cuts of meat allows their plentiful collagen to gelatinize and melt, giving them succulence and transforming their toughness into pull-apart tenderness. (Visit www.sousvidesupreme.com for detailed time and temperature charts.)

Food safety in sous vide cooking

As with all cooking methods, it is important to use clean, fresh ingredients and to work with clean hands and tools on clean surfaces. When cooking food sous vide for immediate consumption—what is termed Cook-Serve—the basic rules of food handling will suffice, because the food will remain hot in the machine until serving and may even get a final high-temperature sear on the barbecue.

Sometimes, especially when entertaining, it is helpful to employ a technique, used widely by restaurant chefs, called Cook-Chill-Hold. In this method, food is vacuum-sealed and cooked to completion in the water oven in advance, and then quick-chilled in an ice water bath for long enough to return it to refrigerator temperature, and out of the so-called "danger zone." The danger zone is the temperature range between 40°F (5°C) and 130°F (54°C) where food-borne bacteria can grow most easily. Even though most of the potentially harmful bacteria will be killed by sous vide cooking, some can protect themselves from the heat by hibernating as dormant forms—called spores—that can blossom again given sufficient time and favorable temperatures.

Quick-chill method

• Quick-chill the warm cooking pouches of food fully submerged in an ice water bath (half ice and half water) for long enough to ensure a quick drop back to refrigerated temperature. Generally this will be the same length as the minimum time required to bring the food to temperature. Add ice or freezer packs as needed.

• Immediately after chilling, either refrigerate or freeze in the pouch. Hold refrigerated pouches of sous vide cooked food for no more than 48 hours; properly frozen food pouches should remain safe for up to one year.

• To ensure safety in holding, particularly with home refrigerators, be sure the refrigerator compartment maintains a temperature below 40°F (5°C), and that the freezer maintains a temperature below 0°F (-17°C).

When you're ready to use the refrigerated or frozen pouches of food, simply drop them in a water bath pre-heated to the original cooking temperature, and heat through. For refrigerated items, the reheating time will be about the same as the time it took to bring the food to target temperature when first cooked—1 hour for a 1-inch (2.54 cm) steak or chicken breast, for example. (Note that while some foods may have been cooked for extended periods of time to tenderize them, the reheating time will only be as long as it takes to bring them to temperature based on thickness.) For frozen items, allow an additional 15 minutes to bring the food to target temperature.

Sealing liquids for sous vide cooking

Preparing liquid-rich foods for sous vide cooking can be accomplished using a chamber vacuum sealer, or by displacing most of the air in a zip-closure pouch by submerging it in water before sealing. Based on a principle first stated by Greek mathematician and physicist Archimedes, here are the simple steps:

1. Fill a zip-closure cooking pouch with food and fluid.

2. Lower the filled pouch, with the zip closure still open, into the water bath (or into a large pot of cooler water, if you prefer.)

3. The weight of the water in the bath or pot will press against the sides of the pouch and force the air out as you lower the zip closure to the surface of the water.

4. Once the zip closure is at the surface and most of the air has been evacuated from the pouch, zip it closed. The zip-sealed pouch should now stay submerged in the water bath.

Measuring recipe ingredients

Because of the precisely controlled temperatures used in sous vide cooking, recipes can be reproduced perfectly time after time. But as with any culinary technique, the success of the recipe also depends on correctly measured ingredients. Different ingredients are measured in different ways and, depending on where you live, using different measuring utensils. In order to ensure that our recipes can be successfully prepared by everyone—whether you live in Des Moines or Tokyo—the ingredient amounts have been specified using both volume and mass (weight).

Mass equivalencies for US volume measuring spoons (teaspoons and tablespoons) are given as UK metric measuring spoons (milliliters). (The same size measuring spoons in Asia are specified in grams.) The volume measure conversions based on cooking utensils are: ¼ teaspoon = 1.25 ml spoon; ½ teaspoon = 2.5 ml spoon; 1 teaspoon = 5 ml spoon; 1 tablespoon = 15 ml spoon.

For liquids, a 1 cup measurement, as well as fractions of a cup, are converted to weights based on 8 fl oz being equivalent to 240 ml, the US FDA standard. Dry volume measures, as well as fluid measurements greater than 1 cup volume, have been converted to actual weights. For example, 1 cup of crumbled Feta cheese weighs 5 oz/150 g, while 1 cup of fine cornmeal weighs 6.3 oz/186 g. A pint of liquid is accurately converted to 16 fl oz/473 ml, not estimated based on 240 ml per cup.

For more easy how-to information on cooking and equipment, complete reference charts for cooking times and temperatures, and additional tips and recipes, visit www.sousvidesupreme.com

More Cookbooks from Paradox Press:

Sous Vide Meat

Sous Vide Poultry

Sous Vide One Pots

Sous Vide Barbecue

Sous Vide Holiday

Sous Vide Cocktails

Sous Vide for the Home Cook